A VALENTINES
breakfast in bed

Mariana Books
Rhyming Series
Book 6 Holidays

By
Roger Carlson

In the middle of February,
there comes a special day;
filled to the brim with joy,
and more love than words can say.

Valentine's Day isn't just about the love,
between a husband and a wife;
it's a day to celebrate all kinds of love,
in every part of life.

So when February 14th dawned,
a morning bright and early;
fourteen year old Aniyah and twelve year old Andres,
had their game plan ready.

"Andres!" hissed Aniyah,
as she poked her brother awake.
"Get up! It's 7a.m.
We have lots of food to make!"

4

"Huuuuh," mumbled Andres,
rolling over to go back to sleep.
"ANDRES, WAKE UP!" hissed Aniyah again.
"Come on, don't make a peep!

5

"Mom and Dad will wake up soon,
we need to get their trays done.
We don't have a minute to spare,
not even a single one!"

The kids snuck towards the kitchen,
and approached their parents' door;
as they tiptoed past their bedroom,
their dad gave a giant snore.

They found two cartons of eggs,
mozzarella and parmesan cheese,
and a stick of butter on a dish.
Then Aniyah said, "Look at these!"

She'd found a big can of baked beans,
and bacon wrapped in foil;
Aniyah took those out to fry
in sizzling cooking oil!

They grabbed four plump buttermilk biscuits,
in a box from the bakery;
jams of every flavor were on the side,
Andres spread them out to see.

They found fresh fruit in a bowl,
bananas, oranges, strawberries and apples that were loose;
Aniyah kept the oranges aside,
to turn them into a sweet, pulpy juice.

They got out a sheet of paper,
and Aniyah sat down with a pen.
"Alright, let's write down dishes," said Aniyah.
"What shall we do first, then?"

Andres said, "Scrambled eggs for sure
and juice to wash it down;
also, bacon, grits, biscuits, and baked beans,
and a bib to save Mom's nightgown!"

Breakfast List :

- Scrambled eggs
- bacon
- grits
- baked beans
- biscuits
- fresh fruit
- moms bib, and
- orange juice.

13

Aniyah looked in the vegetable drawer.
"Oh! We have mushrooms!" Aniyah said,
Andres added mushrooms to the menu,
for their parents to eat in bed.

14

Once they were ready,
they found pots and pans;
they got out dishes, ladles, and spoons,
they had so many grand plans!

Aniyah set two large plates
on a big wooden tray;
she put a flower in a vase,
to brighten up their day!

Andres took the juicer
and squeezed three oranges to go;
he made a jug full of juice,
then he grabbed a tomato.

Aniyah made scrambled eggs,
frying bacon and grits on the side;
Andres roasted mushrooms and tomatoes
and placed them right beside.

Then, they added the four biscuits,
and cut the butter in a long bit,
set cheese slices on a platter,
and added fresh fruit with it.

They arranged the tiny jams
around the two plates;
when they added the baked beans,
everything looked so great!

They grabbed two glasses
and poured orange juice to the brim;
Aniyah made strong coffee as well,
in cups that said "Her" and "Him."

The fruit platter came next,
with chopped bananas, apples, and strawberries;
a dollop of whip cream on the top,
to make everything yummy and merry!

When they were done,
Aniyah lifted the heavy tray;
she waited for Andres to go first,
so he could lead the way.

They climbed up to the first floor
and knocked on their parents' door;
then Andres knocked again,
in case they hadn't heard before.

Mom opened the door,
and saw them standing with a grin;
she broke into a big smile,
and said "Kids! Come in!"

"Happy Valentine's Day!"
Aniyah and Andres chimed;
Mom and Dad devoured the breakfast,
and the food was gone in no time!

"Kids, that was wonderful!" said Dad,
Mom agreed with a smile.
"This has been the best Valentine's Day
we've had in quite a while!"

The four of them stayed in bed
all throughout the day;
Valentine's Day was a great success,
hip hip hooray!

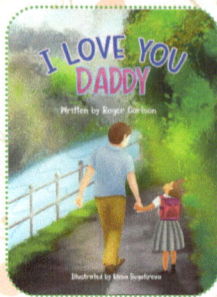

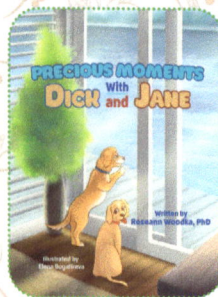

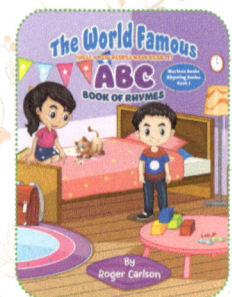

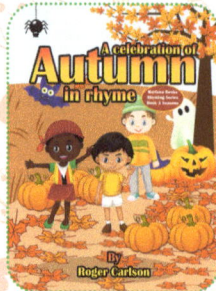

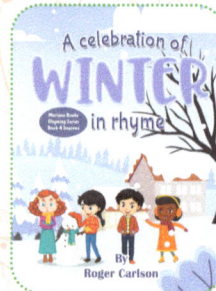

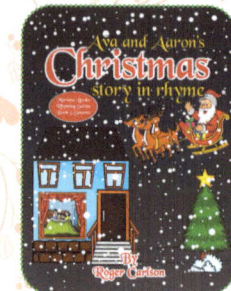

WAYBACK BOOKS

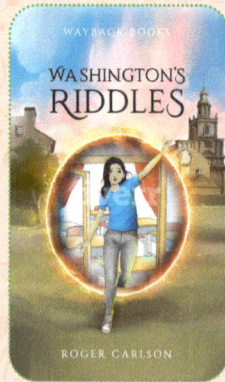

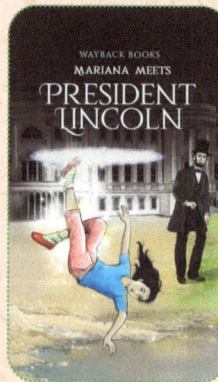

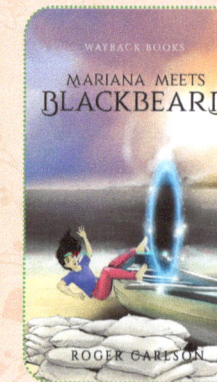

www.ingramcontent.com/pod-product-compliance
Lightning Source LLC
Chambersburg PA
CBHW061051090426
42740CB00002B/110